CONTEMPORARY MUSICAL THEATRE FOR TEENS

YOUNG WOMEN'S EDITION VOLUME 2

31 SONGS FROM 25 MUSICALS

ISBN 978-1-4803-9519-0

HAL•LEONARD® CORPORATION

7777 W. BLUEMOUND RD. P.O. BOX 13819 MILWAUKEE, WI 53213

Visit Hal Leonard Online at
www.halleonard.com

CONTENTS

BELLE
(Reprise)
from Walt Disney's *Beauty and the Beast*

Lyrics by Howard Ashman
Music by Alan Menken

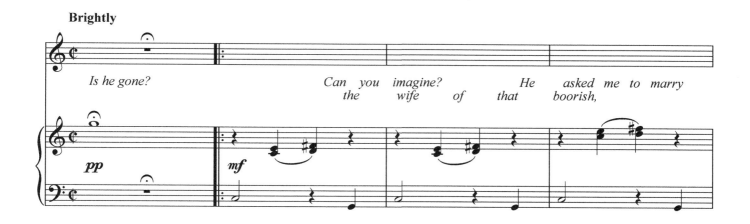

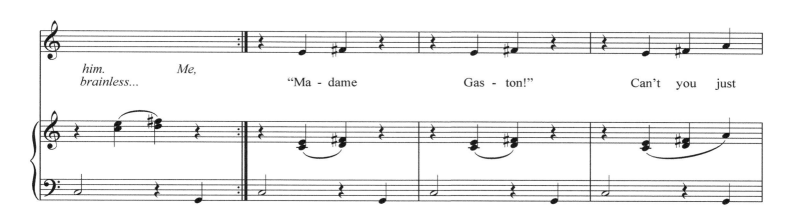

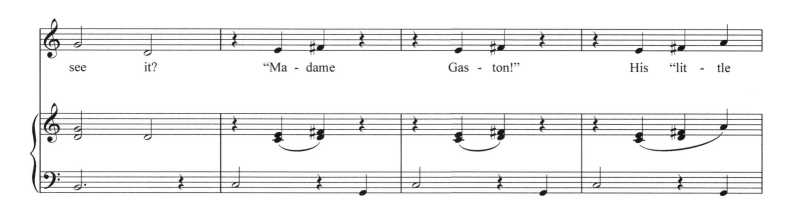

wife." No, sir. Not me! I guar - an -

tee it! I want much more than this pro - vin - cial

life.

cresc.

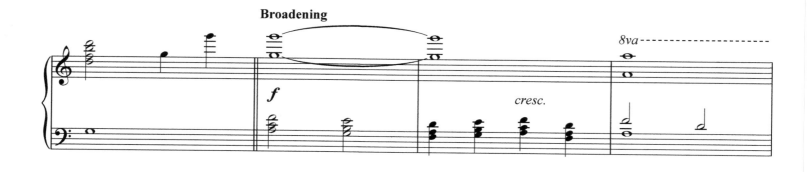

Broadening

f

cresc.

8va

HOME

from Walt Disney's *Beauty and the Beast: The Broadway Musical*

Music by Alan Menken
Lyrics by Tim Rice

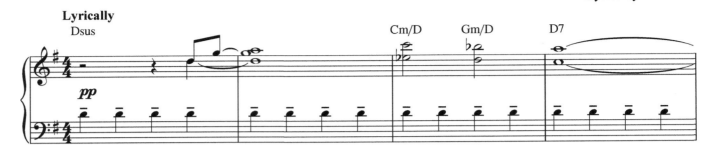

Yes, I made the choice. For Pa-pa, I will stay.

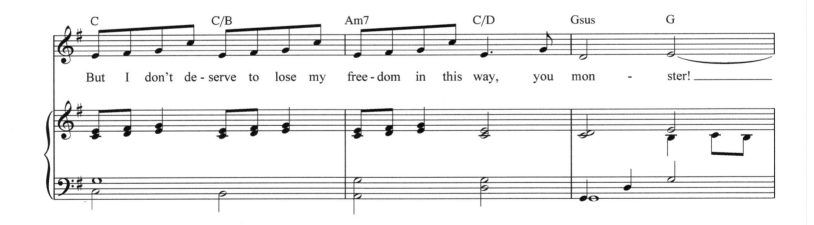

But I don't de-serve to lose my free-dom in this way, you mon - ster! _____

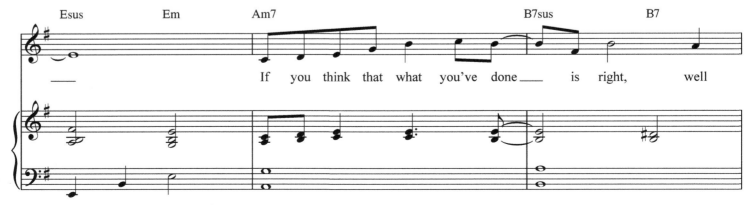

_____ If you think that what you've done _____ is right, well

I KNOW THE TRUTH
from Elton John and Tim Rice's *Aida*

Music by Elton John
Lyrics by Tim Rice

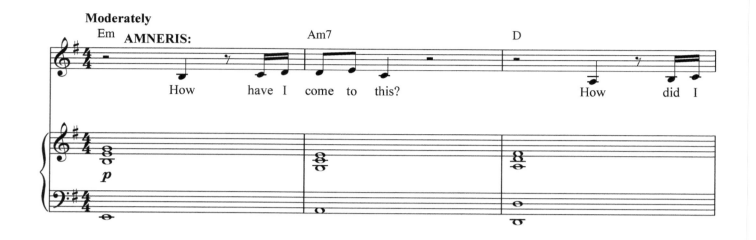

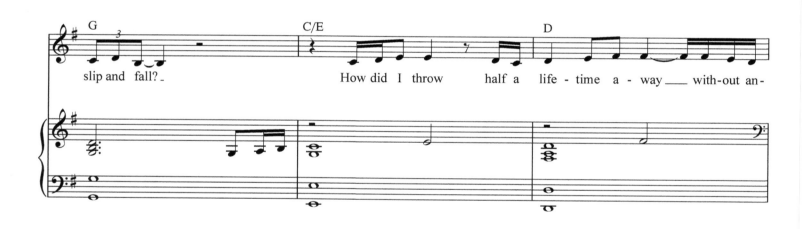

TRYOUTS
from *Bring It On*

Music by Tom Kitt
Lyrics by Amanda Green

Power Ballad (♩ = 72)

SKYLAR:

I re-member my first try-outs, and my sec-ond and third, too, All the fear and ho-ly hell the jud-ges put me through. I felt so be-lit-tled. Man, they put me on the rack. And

21

WE'RE NOT DONE

from *Bring It On*

Music by Tom Kitt
and Lin-Manuel Miranda
Lyrics by Lin-Manuel Miranda
and Amanda Green

DANIELLE:

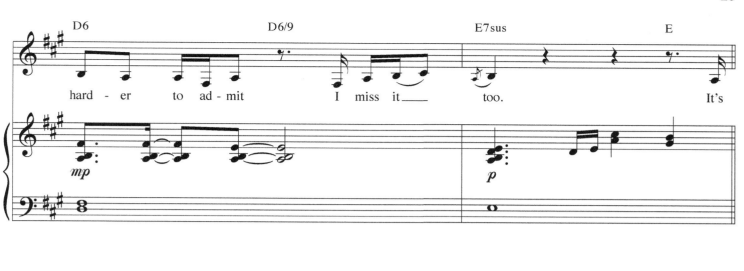

hard - er to ad - mit I miss it____ too. It's

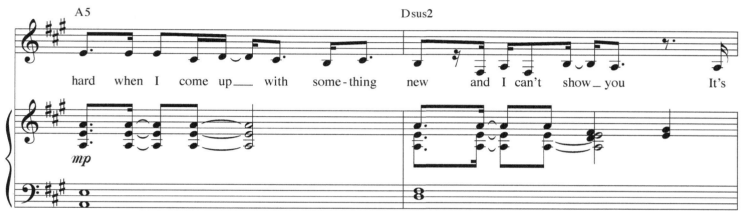

hard when I come up___ with some - thing new and I can't show_ you It's

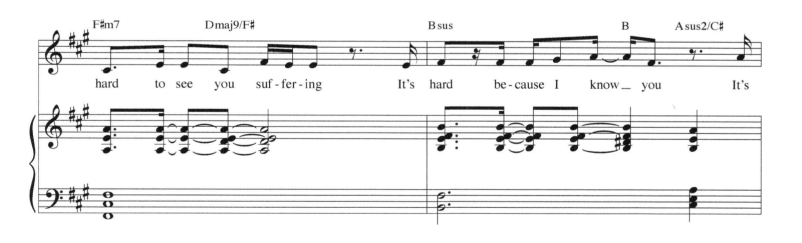

hard to see you suf - fer - ing It's hard be - cause I know_ you It's

hard to find___ for - give - ness, We've said all there is to_ say What

SHOW OFF
from *The Drowsy Chaperone*

Words and Music by Lisa Lambert
and Greg Morrison

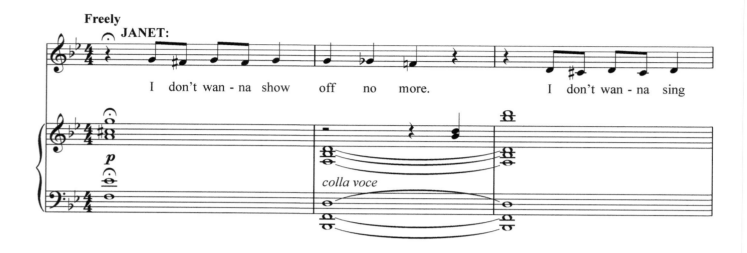

Janet is joined by chorus in this number, edited here as a solo.

Wheee! Please no more at-ten-tion

I've count-ed to ten and I'm

thru. A - dieu You'll nev-er see this...

(she dances)

You'll

GOOD MORNING BALTIMORE
from *Hairspray*

Music by Marc Shaiman
Lyrics by Marc Shaiman and Scott Wittman

Tracy is joined by the chorus in the original number, adapted here as a solo.

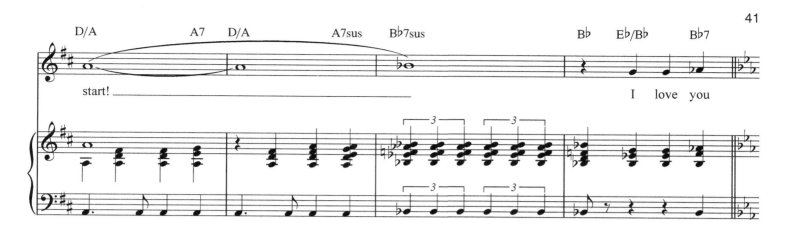

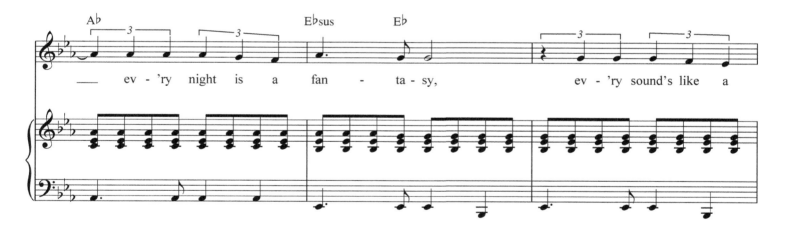

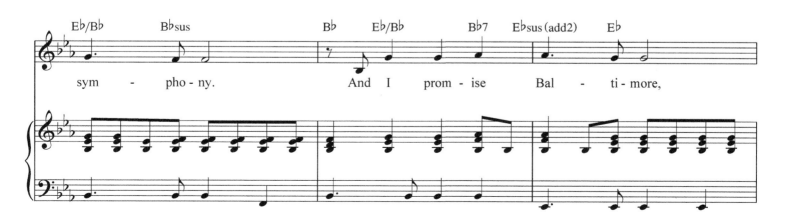

START OF SOMETHING NEW
from the Disney Channel Original Movie *High School Musical*

Words and Music by Matthew Gerrard
and Robbie Nevil

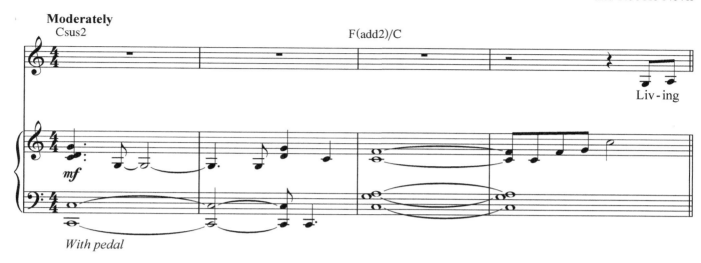

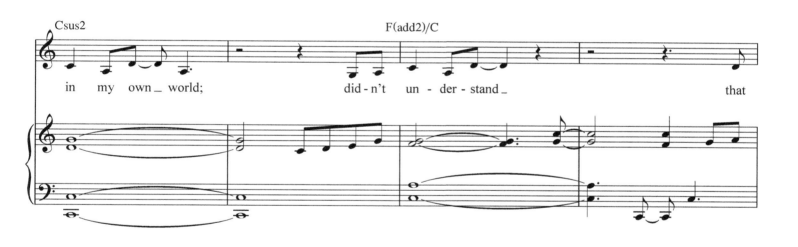

Originally a duet, this song has been adapted for this solo edition.

44

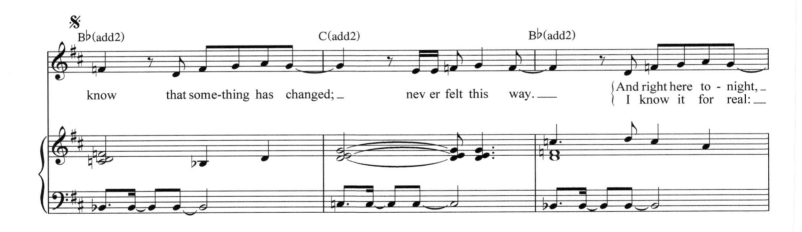

EVERYTHING I KNOW

from *In the Heights*

Music and Lyrics by Lin-Manuel Miranda
Arrangement by Alex Lacamoire and Bill Sherman

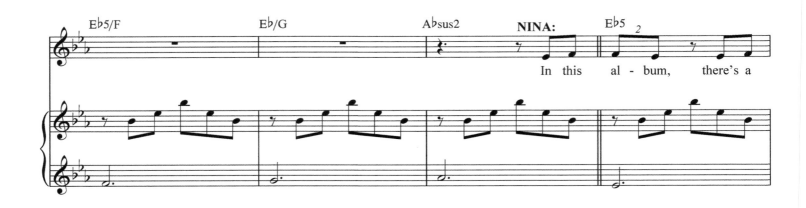

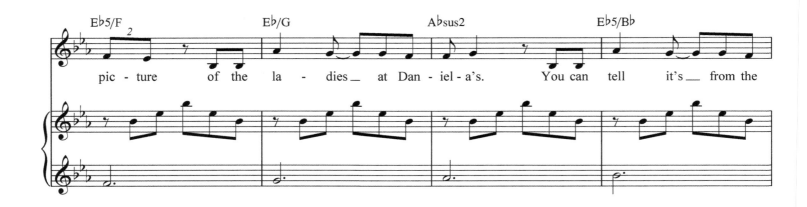

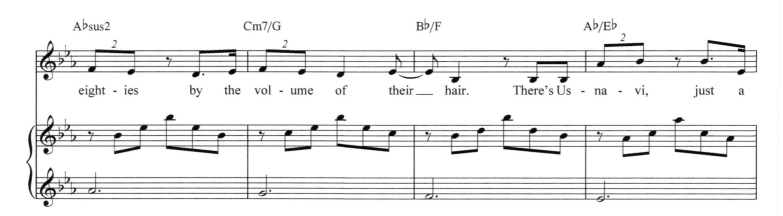

IT WON'T BE LONG NOW

from *In the Heights*

Music and Lyrics by Lin-Manuel Miranda
Arrangement by Alex Lacamoire and Bill Sherman

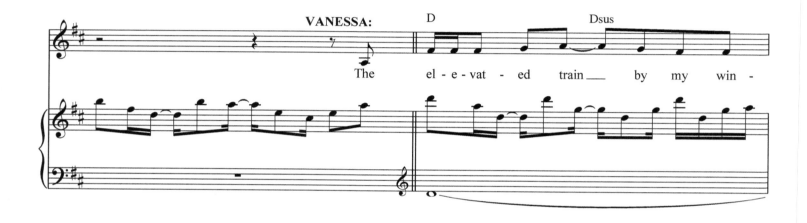

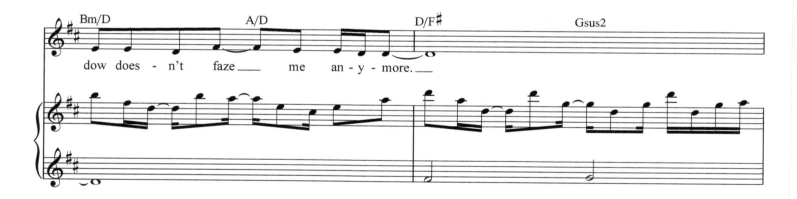

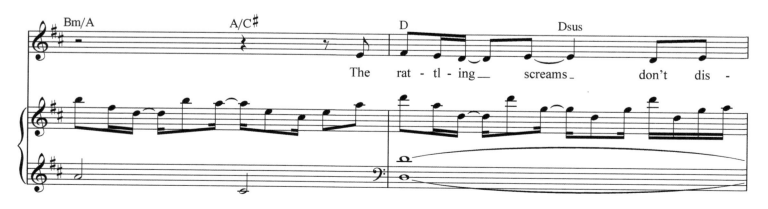

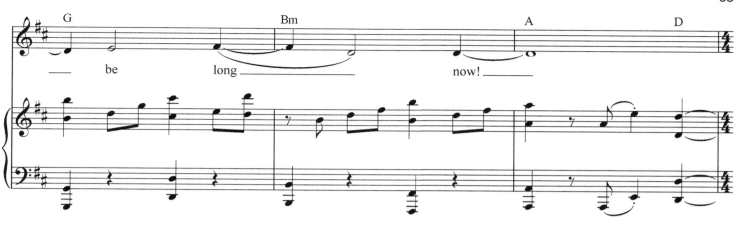

be long _____ now! _____

Tempo I
(♩ = ♩)

With pedal

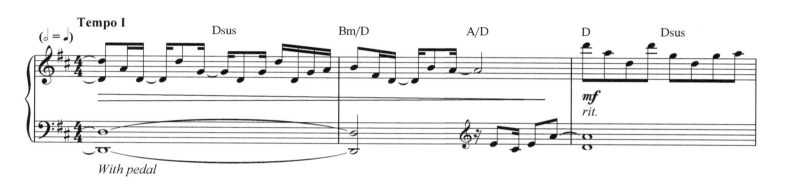

Calmly, poco rubato

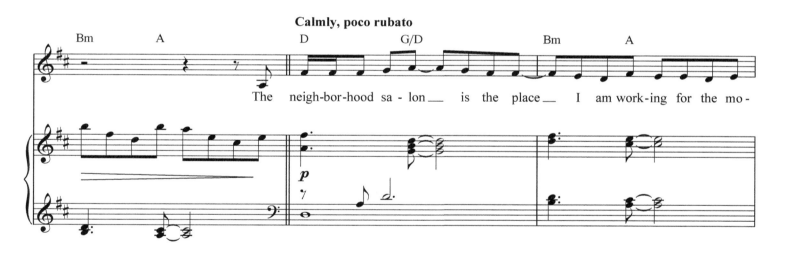

The neigh-bor-hood sa - lon ___ is the place ___ I am work-ing for the mo -

ment. As I cut their ___ hair, ___ la - dies

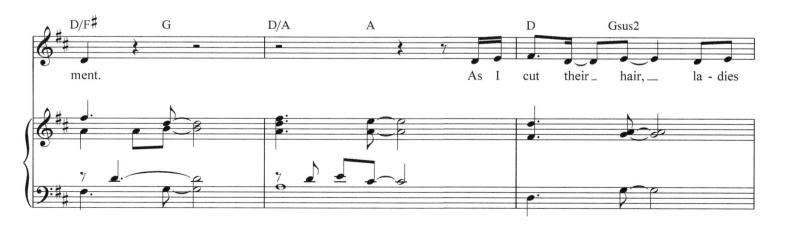

A PART OF THAT

from *The Last Five Years*

Music and Lyrics by
Jason Robert Brown

74

SO MUCH BETTER
from *Legally Blonde*

Music and Lyrics by Laurence O'Keefe
and Nell Benjamin

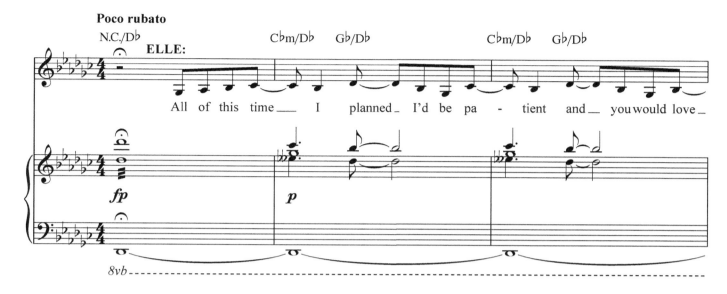

All of this time __ I planned __ I'd be pa - tient and __ you would love __

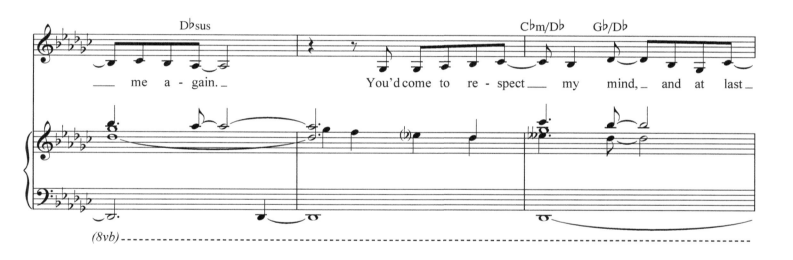

__ me a - gain. __ You'd come to re - spect __ my mind, __ and at last __

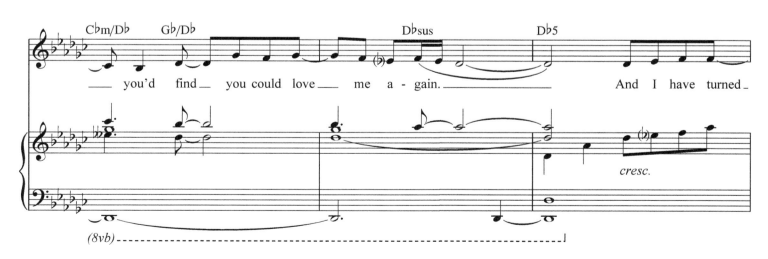

__ you'd find __ you could love __ me a - gain. _____ And I have turned __

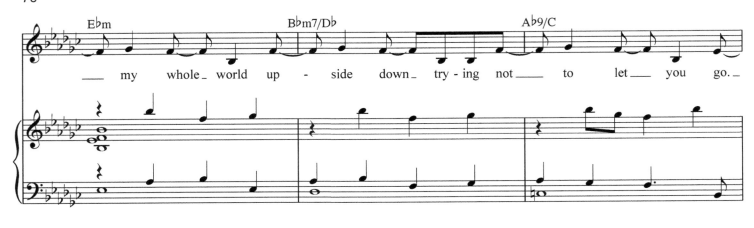

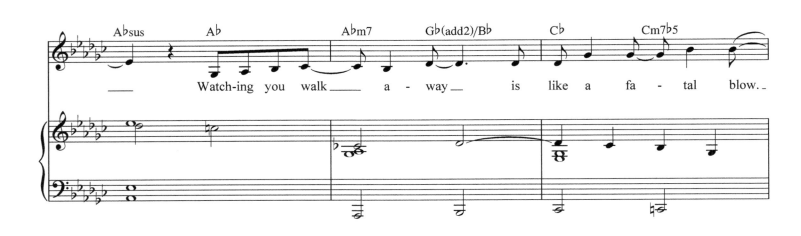

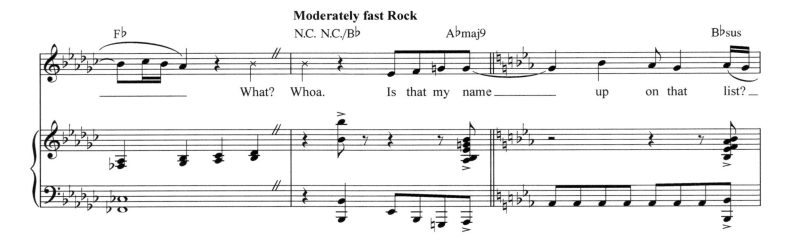

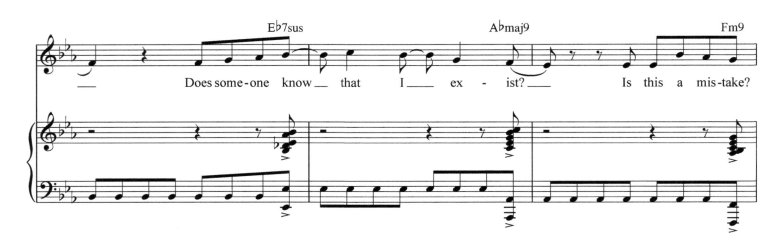

bet-ter jobs __ or big-ger rings. __ I don't have the time to cry.

I'm too bus-y lov-in' my name _____ up on that list! __ Kind of a cool __

__ i - ron - ic twist! __ Who else can I tell? __ Oo, wait, where's my cell?

__ Mom will fall on the floor. __ Hey, Mom! Look at my name __

84

WHIPPED INTO SHAPE

from *Legally Blonde*

Music and Lyrics by Laurence O'Keefe
and Nell Benjamin

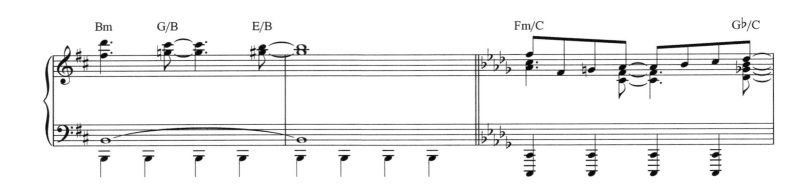

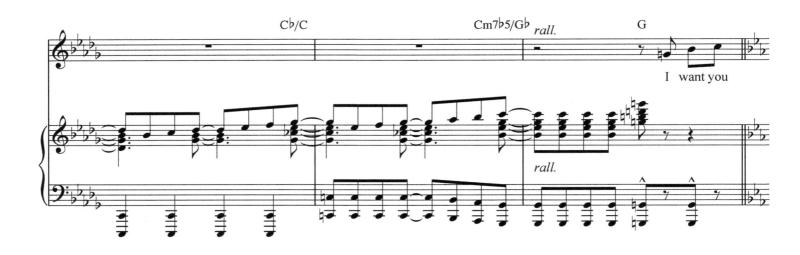

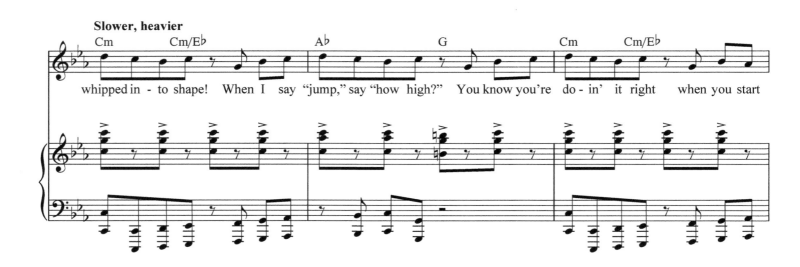

LIVE OUT LOUD
from *A Little Princess*

Music by Andrew Lippa
Lyrics by Brian Crawley

Gentle, but with a strong sense of time

SARA:

I don't want to go____ a - long____ with the crowd.____ Don't want to live____

____ life un - der a cloud.____ Give me some air____ and space____ and the

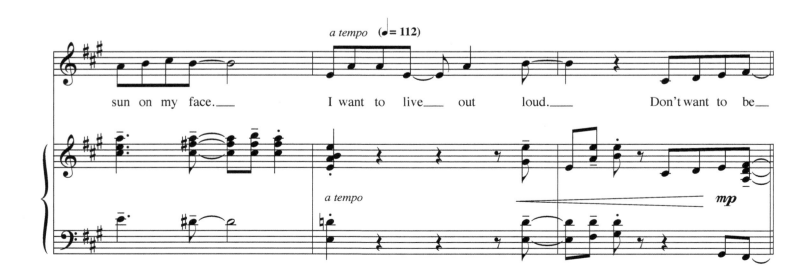

sun on my face.____ I want to live____ out loud.____ Don't want to be____

93

Quasi African Drums

Lyrics:

I want the life they took a-way from me!

If that makes me head - strong, fine. That's a fault I'm glad

is mine. I don't want to go a - long with the crowd.

Don't want my spir - it bro - ken and bowed. Why do I have

to hide___ what I'm feel-ing in-side?___ I want to live___ out loud.___

___ Don't want to be___ a-lone___ in the crowd.___ I on-ly want___

___ what I'm___ not al-lowed.___ Give me the wings___ of a bird,___ I'll be

seen and be heard.   I want to sing when my heart is full.   I want to sing and I want to fly.

same as before

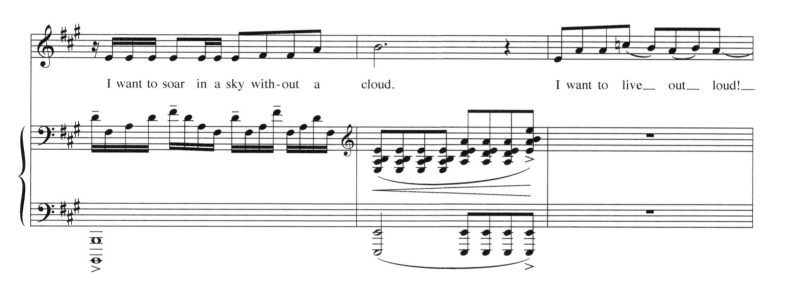

I want to soar in a sky with-out a   cloud.   I want to live__ out__ loud!__

ff

ASTONISHING
from the Broadway Musical *Little Women*

Music by Jason Howland
Lyrics by Mindi Dickstein

105

WAITING FOR LIFE

from *Once on This Island*

Lyrics by Lynn Ahrens
Music by Stephen Flaherty

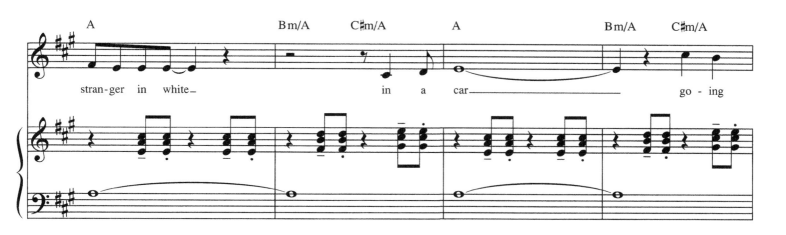

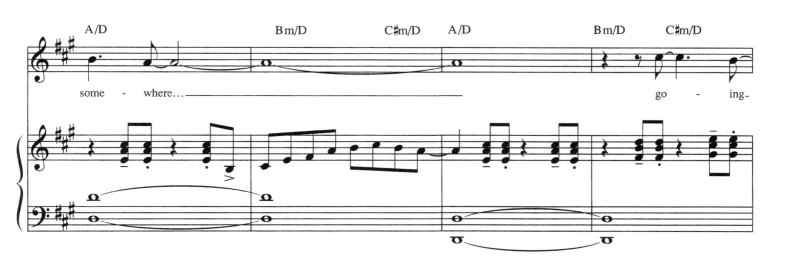

PRACTICALLY PERFECT

from *Mary Poppins*

Music by George Stiles
Lyrics by Anthony Drewe

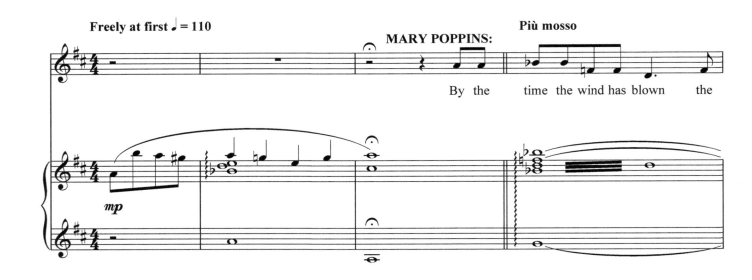

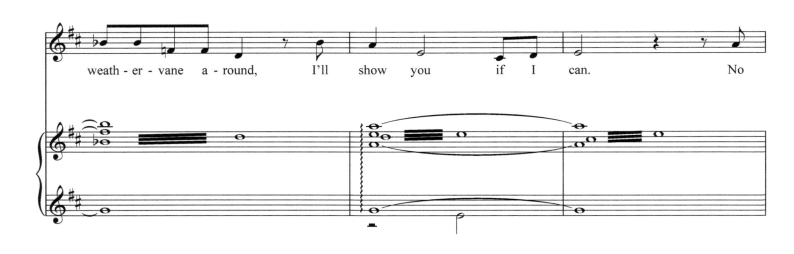

sound. I'm prac-ti-cal-ly per - fect___ from head to

toe. If I had a fault, it would nev-er dare to

show. I'm so prac-ti - cal - ly per-fect in

Poco più mosso

ev - e - ry way.___

Both prim and pro - per and nev - er too stern. _

sempre staccato

f *p*

Well ed - u - cat - ed, yet will - ing to learn. _

I'm clean and hon - est, my man - ner re - fined, _

and I wear shoes of the sen - si - ble kind. _

Un - can - ny nan - nies are hard to find._____

U - nique, yet meek, un - speak - a - bly kind.

I'm prac - ti - cal - ly per - fect,_____ not slight - ly soiled,

run - ning like an en - gine that's just been fresh - ly oiled.

FIND YOUR GRAIL

from *Monty Python's Spamalot*

Lyrics by Eric Idle
Music by John Du Prez and Eric Idle

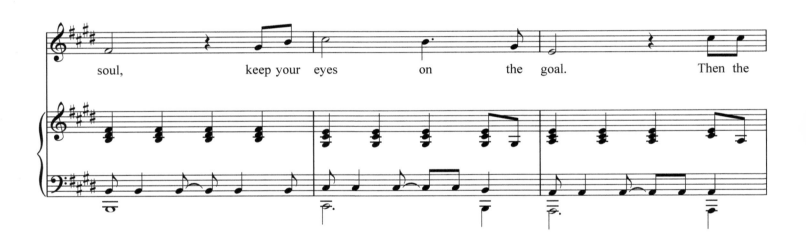

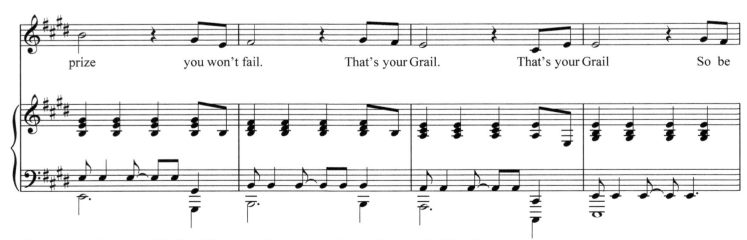

This is a parody pop/rock ballad. The original cast singer imitated many clichéd styles in the song.

I KNOW IT'S TODAY
from *Shrek the Musical*

Words and Music by David Lindsey-Abaire
and Jeanine Tesori

The song, first sung by Young Fiona then Teen Fiona, then the adult Fiona, has been adapted as a solo.
Original key is one step higher.

I'M NOT AFRAID OF ANYTHING

from *Songs for a New World*

Music and Lyrics by
Jason Robert Brown

143

So let__them call.____ And watch__them fall.___

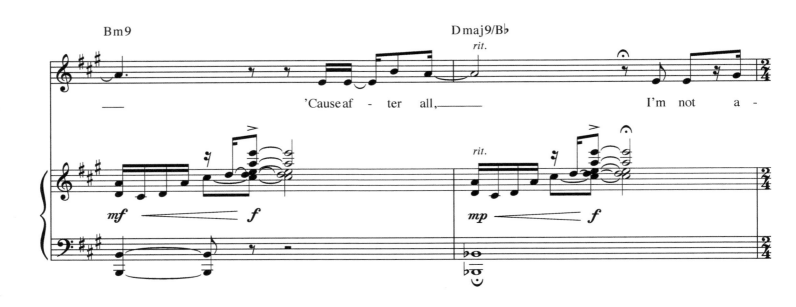

__ 'Cause af - ter all,_____ I'm not a -

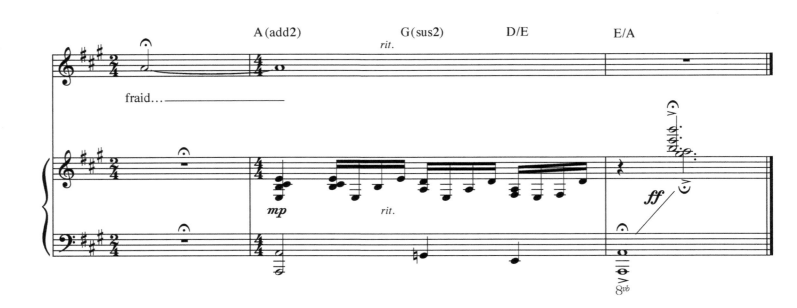

fraid..._____

THIS PAGE HAS INTENTIONALLY BEEN LEFT BLANK TO FACILITATE PAGE TURNS.

WHISPERING

from *Spring Awakening*

Music by Duncan Sheik
Lyrics by Steven Sater

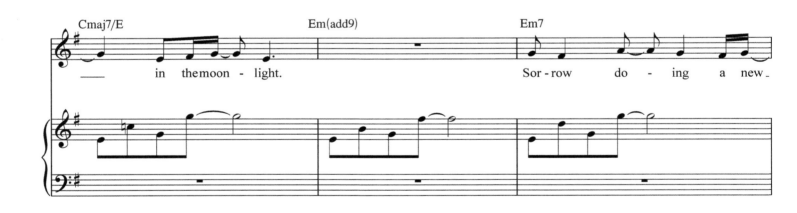

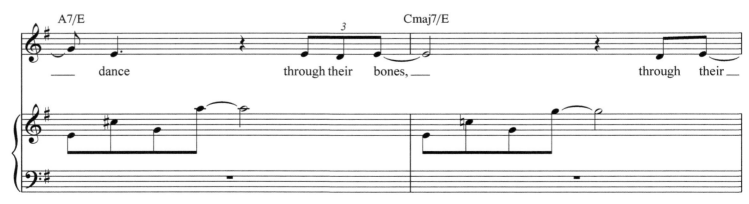

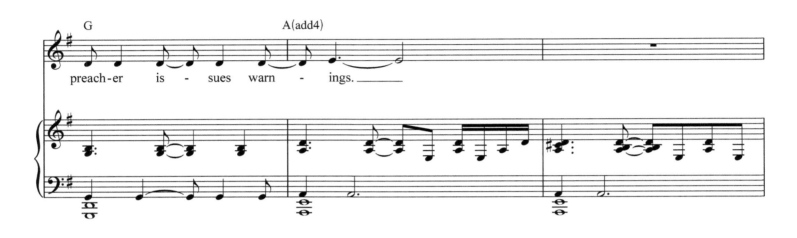

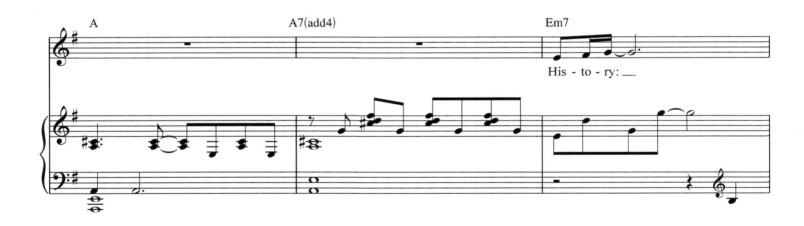

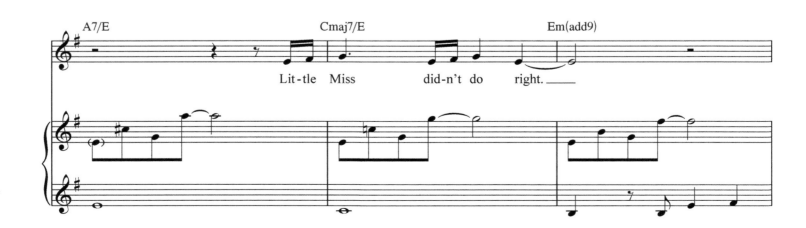

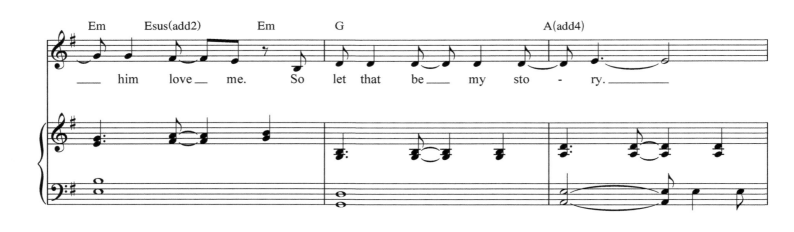

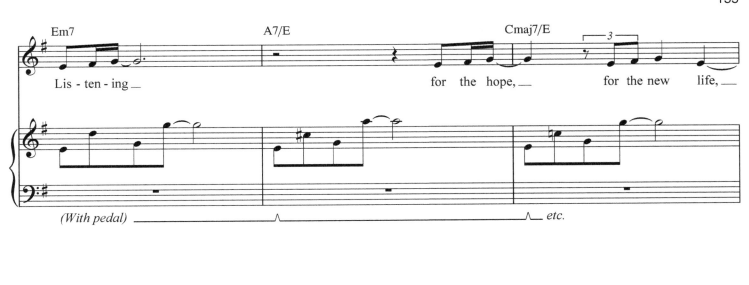

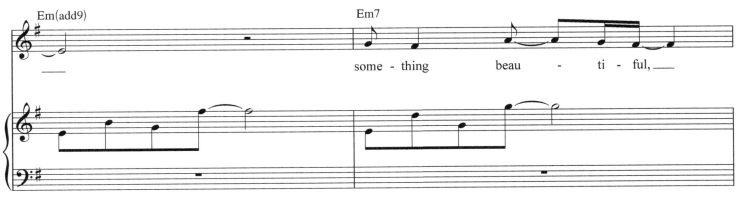

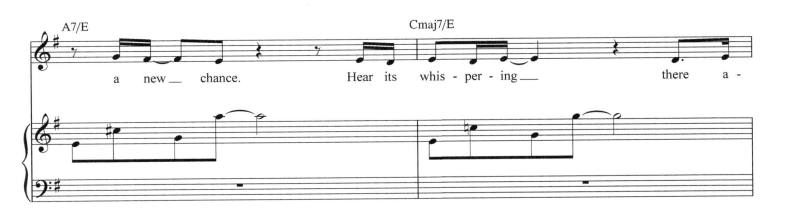

THE LAMEST PLACE IN THE WORLD
from the Broadway Musical *13*

Music and Lyrics by
Jason Robert Brown

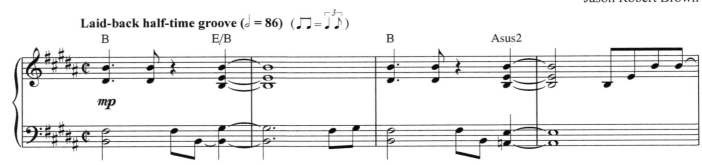

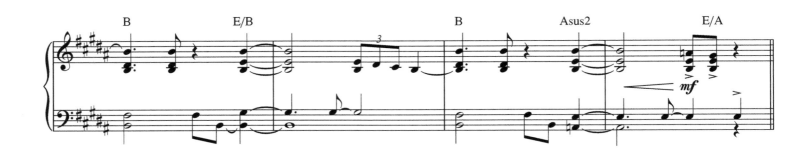

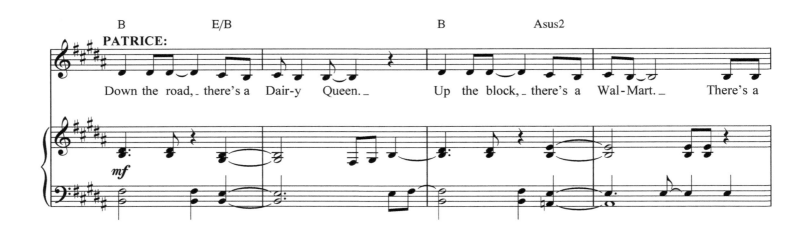

PATRICE:
Down the road, there's a Dair-y Queen. Up the block, there's a Wal-Mart. There's a

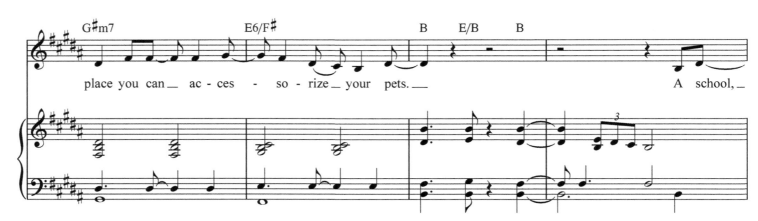

place you can ac-ces-so-rize your pets. A school,

alternative lyric: stu-pid

lam - est place ___ in ___ the world. ___ But I'm pret-ty sure ___ It's

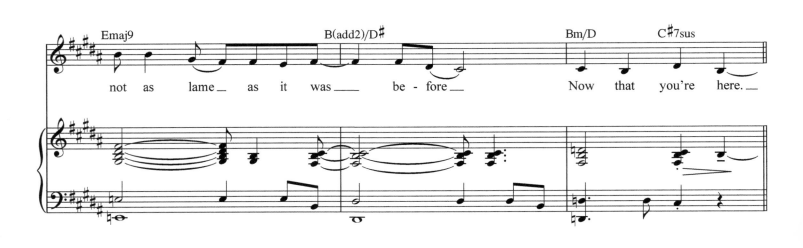

not as lame ___ as it was ___ be - fore ___ Now that you're here. ___

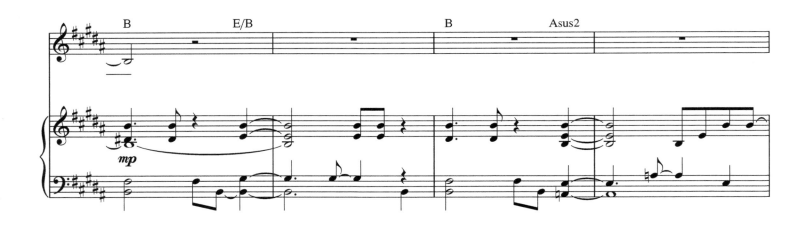

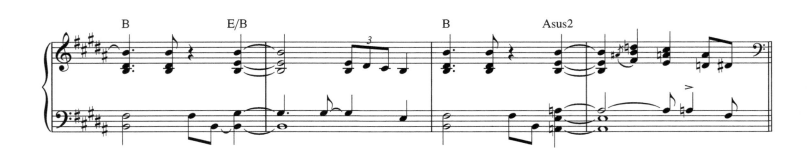

COME TO YOUR SENSES

from *tick, tick... BOOM!*

Words and Music by
Jonathan Larson

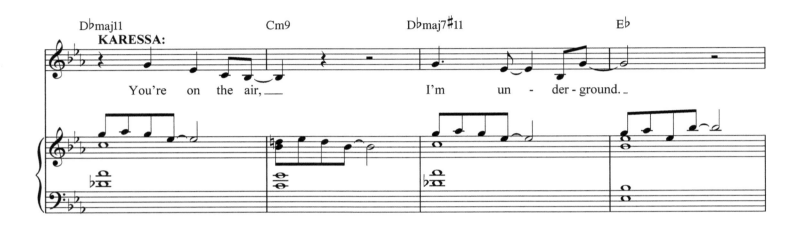

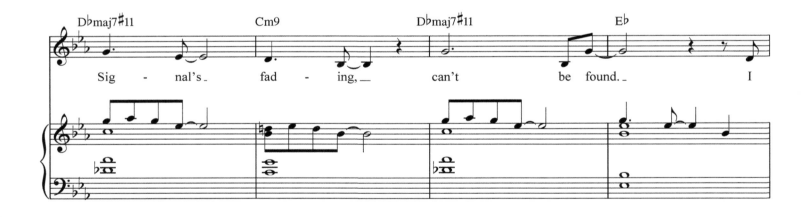

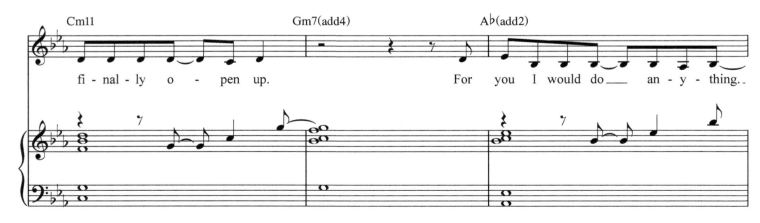

I SPEAK SIX LANGUAGES

from *The 25th Annual Putnam County Spelling Bee*

Words and Music by
William Finn

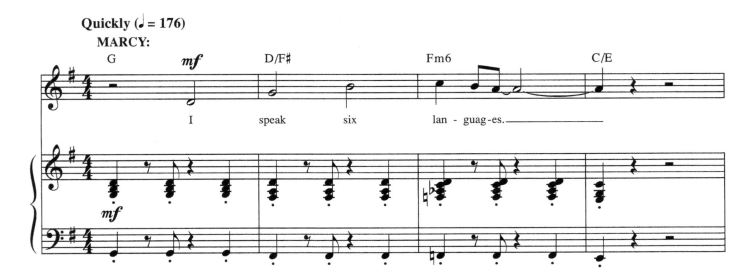

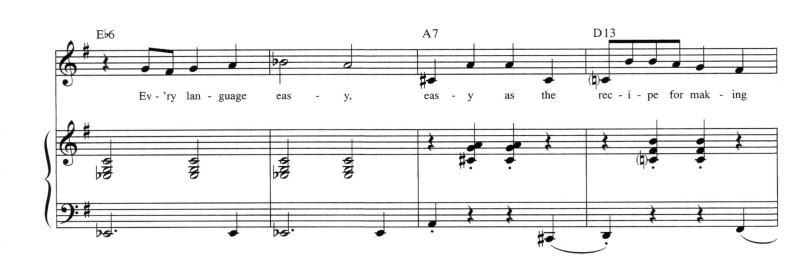

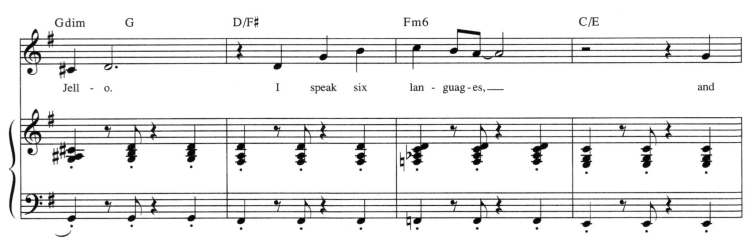

MAYBE I LIKE IT THIS WAY

from *The Wild Party*

Words and Music by
Andrew Lippa

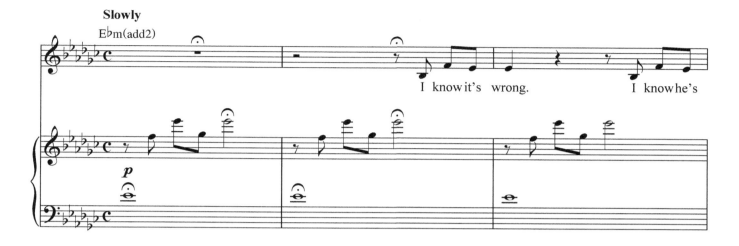

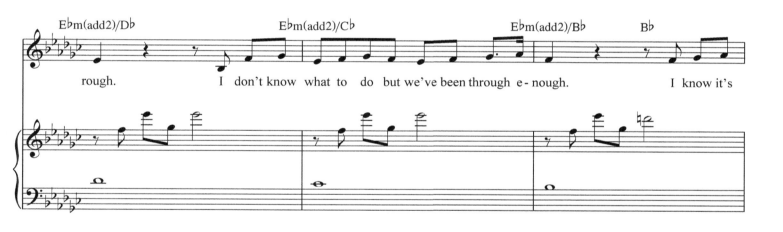

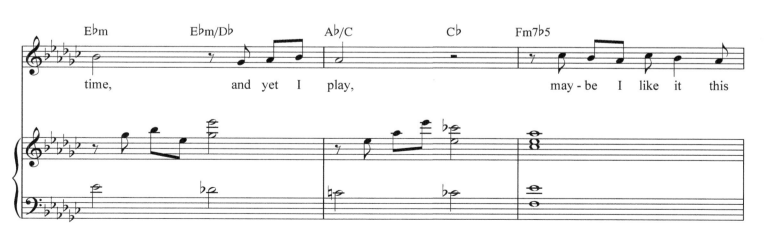

FOLLOW YOUR HEART

from *Urinetown*

Music and Lyrics by Mark Hollmann
Book and Lyrics by Greg Kotis

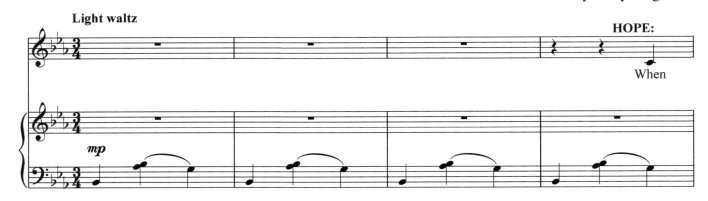

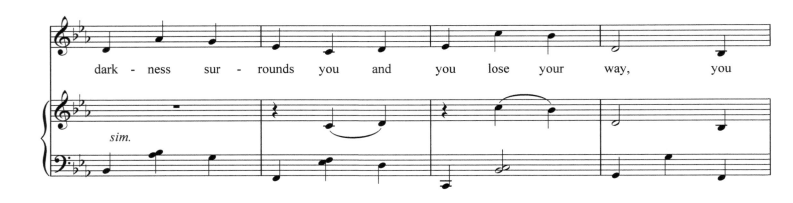

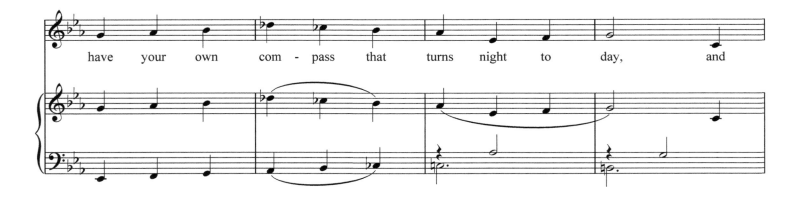

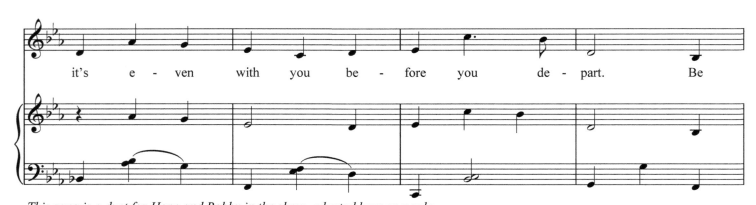

This song is a duet for Hope and Bobby in the show, adapted here as a solo.

185

still, hear it beat - ing, it's lead - ing you: fol - low your

heart.

rit.   *a tempo*

We all want a world filled with peace and with

mp

joy, with plen - ty of wa - ter for each girl and

boy. That bright, shin - ing world is just wait - ing to

start. No mean - ness or sor - row, just clean - ness to -

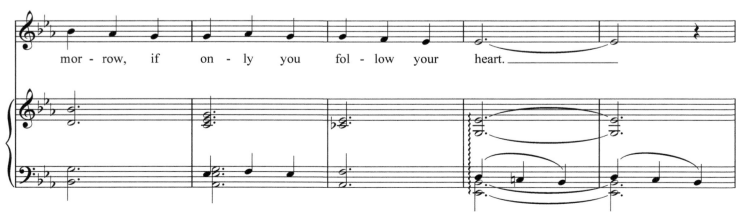

mor - row, if on - ly you fol - low your heart.

rit.　　　　a tempo

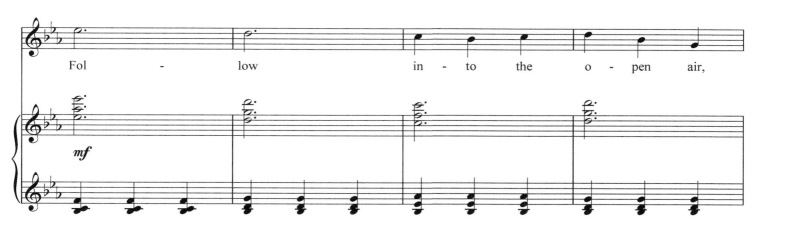

Fol - low　　　in - to the o - pen air,

mf

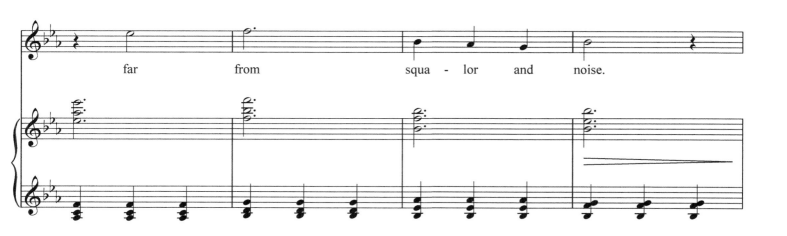

far　from　squa - lor and noise.

Fol - low, some - one is

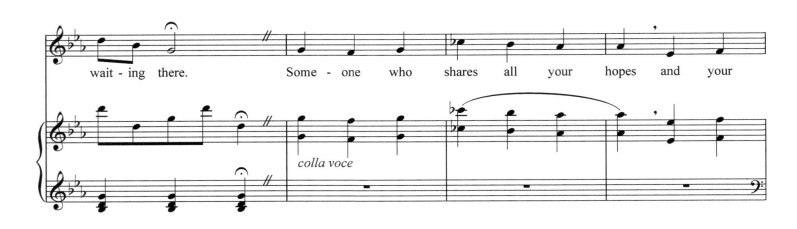

wait - ing there. Some - one who shares all your hopes and your

colla voce

a tempo

joys. Some day I'll meet

a tempo

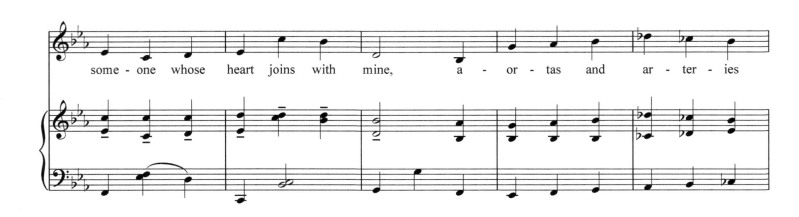

some - one whose heart joins with mine, a - or - tas and ar - ter - ies

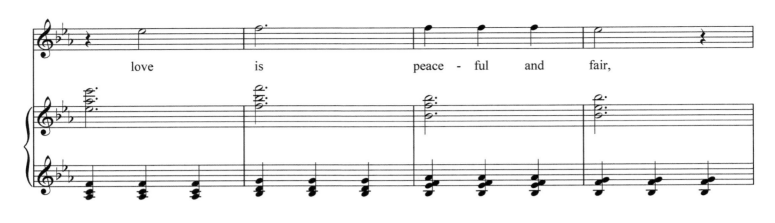

love   is   peace - ful   and   fair,

poco rit.

Love   can   creep   up   so   sud - den - ly;

poco rit.

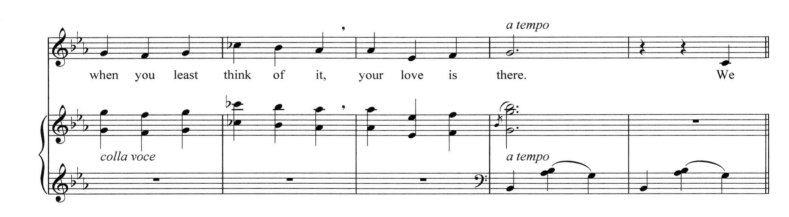

a tempo

when you least think of it, your love is there. We

colla voce   *a tempo*

all want a world filled with peace and with joy, with plen - ty of

f

POPULAR
from the Broadway Musical *Wicked*

Music and Lyrics by
Stephen Schwartz

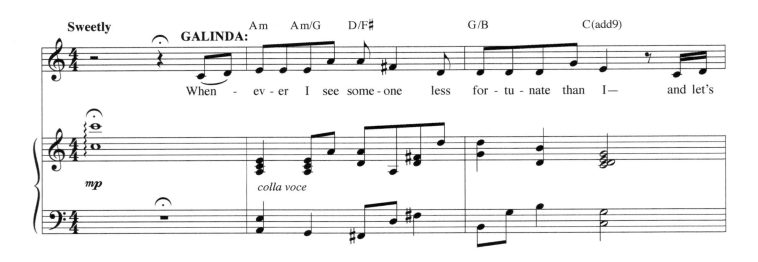

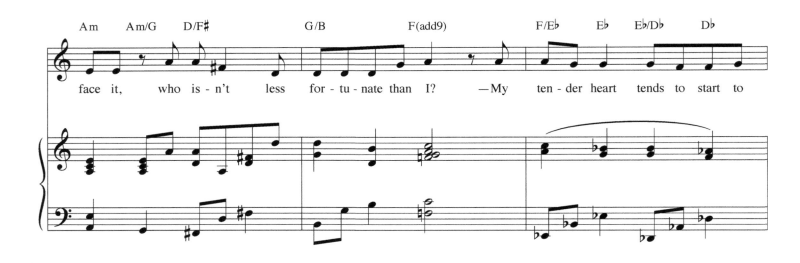

THE WIZARD AND I
from the Broadway Musical *Wicked*

Music and Lyrics by
Stephen Schwartz

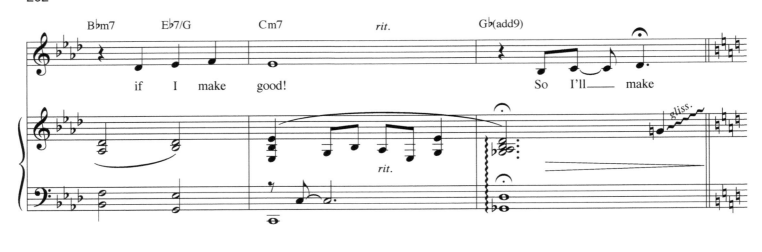

Pulsing with excitement

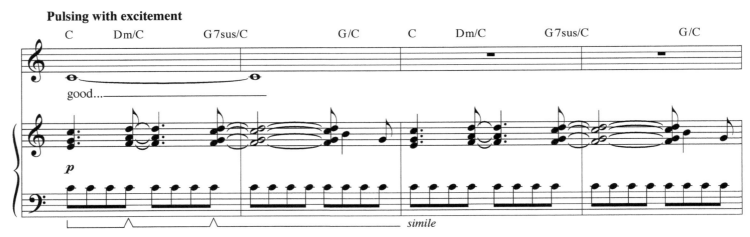

good...

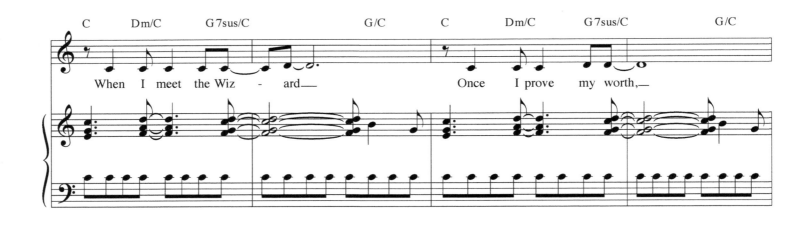

When I meet the Wiz - ard___   Once I prove my worth,___

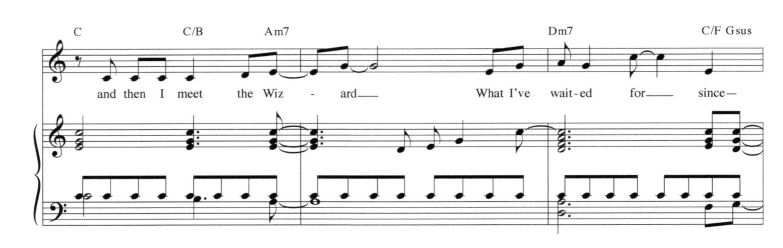

and then I meet the Wiz - ard___   What I've wait-ed for___ since___

FINDING WONDERLAND
from the Broadway Musical *Wonderland*

Music by Frank Wildhorn
Lyrics by Jack Murphy

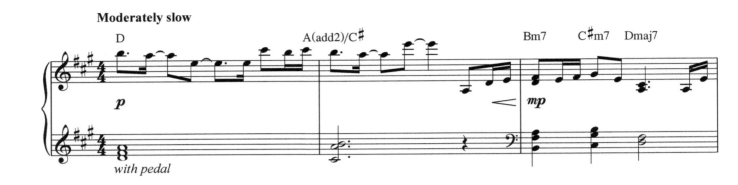

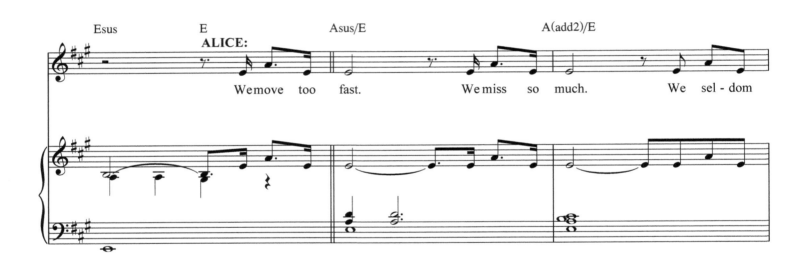

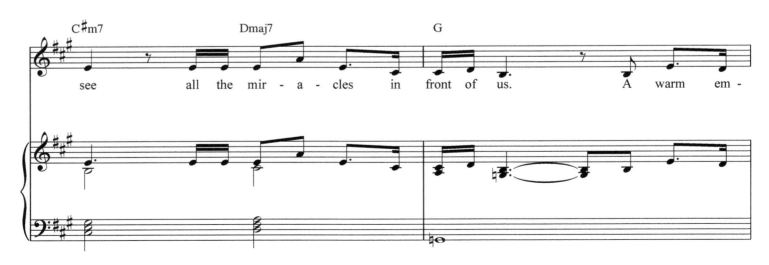

ONCE MORE I CAN SEE

from the Broadway Musical *Wonderland*

Music by Frank Wildhorn
Lyrics by Jack Murphy

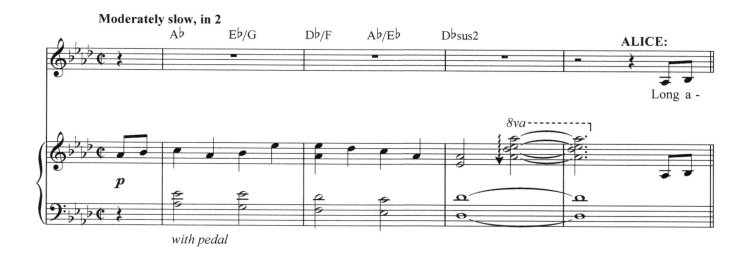

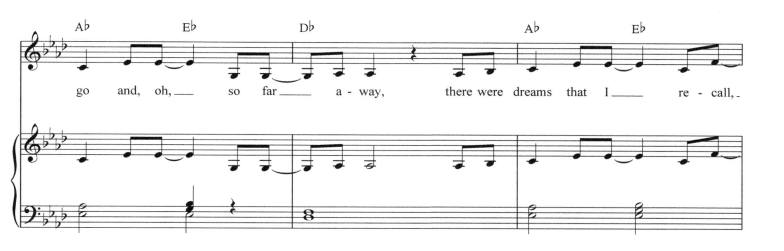

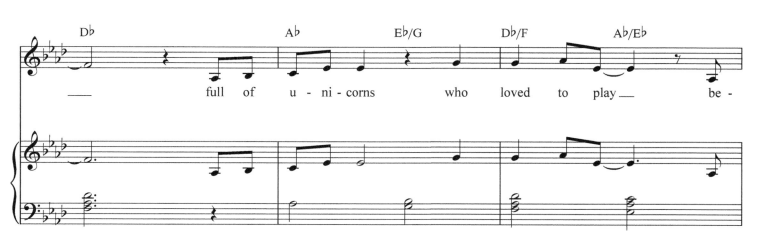

220

223

MY NEW PHILOSOPHY

from *You're a Good Man, Charlie Brown*

Music and Lyrics by
Andrew Lippa

SALLY: *Spoken (before the vamp): "Why are you telling me?" (beat) I like it.*

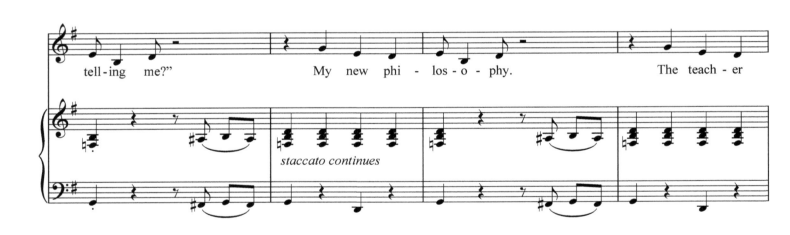

The song is a duet for Sally and Schroeder. The composer created this solo edition for publication.